# Ponds, Tonzs and Boorts

## Tales from the Chesterfield Canal

### by David Bownes

Dedicated to The Boatmen and Maintenance Men
of the Chesterfield Canal from who I learnt so much.

**Ponds** (Pounds) The water between locks
**Tonzs** The local term for a bend in the canal
**Boorts** (Boats)

*A Chesterfield Canal boat crosses Lincoln's Brayford Pool*

3

# Index

| | |
|---|---|
| Foreword | 5 |
| The start | 6 |
| The Clarks | 7 |
| The Walkers | 10 |
| Blaggy | 14 |
| The Chambers Family | 16 |
| John Macfarland | 20 |
| P Hindley and Son | 21 |
| Cliftons | 23 |
| Mrs Foster | 25 |
| Herbert Cook | 27 |
| Charlie and Freda Mitchell | 28 |
| Bill Ledger | 31 |
| Herbert Bagshaw | 33 |
| Top Lock Folks | 34 |
| Richard Furley and Co Ltd | 36 |
| The Manchester, Sheffield and Lincolnshire Railway Company's Canals | 38 |
| The end and a new beginning | 41 |
| Pounds and Turns | 45 |
| Acknowledgements | 53 |
| Friends of Dawn Rose | 53 |

Copyright © Chesterfield Canal Trust Ltd. 2018

All rights reserved. No parts of this publication may be reproduced or transmitted, in any form or by any means, without permission.

Published by Chesterfield Canal Trust Ltd
22, Works Road, Hollingwood, Chesterfield, S43 2PF
www.chesterfield-canal-trust.org.uk

Email: publicity@chesterfield-canal-trust.org.uk
Tel: 01246 477569

ISBN No. 978-1-9999465-0-0

A CIP catalogue record for this book is available from the British Library

# Foreword

My first encounter with David Bownes was through his brother Gerald in the early 1960's when I was asked along to help on one of the boats David had built, i.e., "Lorna". David along with some friends was taking passengers along the Chesterfield Canal from Drakeholes to Wiseton for a charge of a shilling for adults and sixpence for children. A horse was used to pull the boat along for each trip and we were busy in the summer!

David's other boat was "Marion", similar to "Lorna" being heavily built in timber and was moored in Worksop Company yard just below Town Lock.

In 1964, David, Gerald, Reg and Mary Richardson and family said they were moving "Marion" down to Drakeholes from Worksop and would I like to come as crew? This boat move started my life-long interest in boating and the Chesterfield Canal. "Marion" was horse-drawn and I was sometimes in charge of the "thurrup line" which controlled the movement between the boat and the horse.

Each Sunday in summer, the boats did passenger trips from Drakeholes, "Lorna" up to Wiseton and "Marion" being outboard powered through Drakeholes tunnel down to Gringley. Gerald Bownes and I crewed these latter trips.

When it was decided that a Chesterfield boat could be built, David was the only person that Richard Allsopp and I knew to ask. Without David the boat would not have been constructed, his description of each stage of the building of "Dawn Rose", the timber, the shape, the fixings, the sealing and the finish display his thorough knowledge and carpentry skills. The boat remains an accurate and lasting achievement for David and the "Dawn Rose" builders and is there for spectators to admire the hand-built piece of waterway history.

Harry Richardson

5

# The start

My association with the Chesterfield Canal goes back over sixty five years to 1949, possibly from seeing Pearce Hindley and his son Joe taking the last load of coal from Shireoaks pit to Walkeringham brick works on narrow boat 'Ruth' and steam dredger 'Joan' operated by Mr Hunter from Retford loco spot dredging from Priorswell bridge to Kilton Top lock after which it was taken stern first to Osberton wharf to await scrapping.

As my interest developed I wanted more than biking along the road to West Stockwith. I wanted a boat and the best way to get one was build one. As an apprentice at Oates wood yard in Worksop one of the jobs I was given was making steam proof wooden cabinets and wooden boiling tanks. Walter Chambers and his son William, two very honest men and cousins to the ' boaty' Chambers family all coming from the Retford, area sold me second hand wagon bottoms and split them for free. A barrel of tar cost five pounds from Staveley plus a pound to collect.

When I came to put the boat in the cut I was advised by Herbert Cooke, the dragline driver, to seek advice from Albert Walker, a time served shipwright working on the 'cut' as a carpenter. He told me everything was wrong, but if I listened, he would teach me. The next boat was a success. I was able to team up with Reg Richardson, a well Worksop horseman and we started running horse drawn boat trips from Drakeholes basin to Wiseton gardens and Bracebridge to Osberton lock.

*Horse Boat Marion at Osberton Turnover bridge*

# The Clarks

I rented half an acre of land at Kilton Top lock from the Osberton estate at fifty shillings a year to be paid on Boxing Day. It was called Crow Wood gardens; ideal to side slip a boat. As I got into building what would become my first successful boat I started getting a visitor on Saturday afternoons after he had closed his pub, the Manton Inn. Harry Clark, the older brother of Ernest Clark who wrote of his life on the boats in his book 'Upgate and Downgate.' Harry in his boating days was known as 'Son' Clark. He told me he did about three years boating and got fed up with the 'up to the knees in sludge, never at home and always skint.' He went to Manton pit and when not working taught himself to play the piano and learn ballroom dancing. He must have been good as he was also teaching and playing the piano at the Unicorn PH in Worksop. 'Son' was also blessed with a talented daughter Norma who sang with the 'Blue Rockets.'

When he worked for his dad their boats were 'Forest King' and 'Forest Queen' both scrapped in Worksop timber basin. Two of the later boats, 'Albion' and 'Lilian' were left at Godley and Gouldings wharf on Eastgate Worksop. When traffic ended they were pulled from the cut by Stan Pickering with their Unipower timber tractor breaking in half during the operation.

When we launched my first boat Harry brought a pint of Double Diamond which he divided into thirds using nip glasses and recited a rhyme that I will always remember

> *'Here's to thee Jinny Hurn*
> *And little men of Wroot*
> *Drink thy fill and do not kill*
> *The men us wek this boort*

The first glass is poured into the water at the stern, the rhyme recited and a small mirror thrown into the cut. A second glass is poured, never thrown, onto the head of the boat and blessed for success. The final third is given to the builder who presents the owner with a pennant.

Jinny Hurn is a water boggart from the Isle of Axholme. Her name is used by a nasty bend on the River Trent and as the narrow boats don't have taff rails the exposed steering position leaves only the tiller to hang onto. A movement forward could pull the tiller from the mortice in the elum and the boatman would be thrown in the water.

I called in Harry's pub odd Saturday dinners and met his brother Billy. His regular job prior to the war was two loads of coal a week from Shireoaks pit to Smith's Albion mills and to unload. They both visited my boat, told me how to 'strap the gate,' the use of 'for-ups' (thurrups) and opening the top gate with the horse and haulage line.

They both related a story from their father of the Galloping Horses of Clayworth common. They said it was the death coach driven by the Grim Reaper. If you heard it coming it either took you or turned your hair white. They both said they had never heard it. Years later I met Harry in retirement and he said how sorry he was that I was forced off the cut and how proud he had been after so many years to steer a horse drawn boat again.

*One of Harry Clark's Sunday school outings to Greenmile*

*The White Hart PH at Clayworth, now headquarters of The Retford and Worksop Boat Club*

# The Walkers

Albert Walker, born and bred in West Stockwith was ready to finish school, but jobs were scarce and his father did not want him at Morris's chemical works. His older brother was a turner at Newell's but they had no vacancies. His father was visited by one William Tomlinson, the local shipwright who lived at ferry landing. Albert's sister May was the village school mistress and William wanted some out of hour's tuition for his son Billy who was two years older than Albert. William wanted Billy to inherit his empire. He did not want to pay for the tuition as he always said 'its parting that makes you without'.

Albert's dad said, my daughter will teach Billy but you give my lad a job. William said timber prices were going up and trade was bad and he was on his way to the poor house. Albert's dad stood his ground and Albert got a seven year indentured apprenticeship starting in 1910.

The yard employed five men and two boys. They had a blacksmiths shop, a Crossley gas engine, a narrow band saw, a big circular saw bench and a saw pit.

William bought second hand beams from Keadby Bridge when the new one was built. They cut them into strokes in the saw pit, built a narrow boat and sold it as new!

The main supplier of timber to the yard was Newsums of Gainsborough. The yard built keels, 'coggies' and narrow boats plus stowers, boat hooks and all types of wooden parts.

William was also Furley's agent, in charge of the wharf, and a ships' husband.

*New gate for West Stockwith lock at Worksop yard*

*Hooke's detachable motor*                    *Harold Walker (left)  Albert Walker (right)*

When WW1 broke out the ladies of the village told all young men to join up. Billy, now out of his time, joined the Royal Navy. Albert was twenty in 1916 and the ladies badgered him to join up. William would not release him from his apprenticeship however.

The same year Albert had to convert a change boat into a motor boat. He had to reverse the cabins with living cabin forward and fit the stove and remove the elum. Two days were allowed and the work was paid for by the War Department including fitting Hook's Patent Detachable Motor. It arrived on a steam wagon from Birmingham with a works fitter and soldiers under the command of an NCO. The soldiers badgered Albert to join up again. William again said no.

The motor was fitted over where the hatch was. It had an electric start and ran on paraffin. They set off on a trial to Cockings winding hole at Walkeringham. At Misterton Low lock the chimney casing caught fire, the trial was aborted and the motor deemed too clumsy to operate easily. The boat was changed back but the WD would not pay extra so the new chimney hole was never filled in and had to be kept covered.

Six months before he was twenty one Albert again planned to join up and William said that if he came back to the yard he would be on a nineteen year olds rate.

He joined the Royal Flying Corps and was sent to Reading to train as a rigger at Huntley and Palmer's biscuit factory that had been taken over for aircraft production. After training he went by ship to Boulogne and then by Crossley truck to the airfield looking after 'Harry Tates' SE 8s. He was delayed after Armistice as new aircraft kept arriving and they had to burn them.

On return to Tomlinson's he completed his time, aged twenty three. William kept his word. Young Billy was back from the Navy and was now running things but trade was falling away and new boats elsewhere were now being built of metal or composite construction. Billy said to Albert, stick with me and we will have the best yard in England. He built a slipway and winch that could pull a keel out and started to concrete the yard without using hardcore!

Ben Barlow, the canal inspector offered Albert a job as canal carpenter and he took it. So Albert came to Worksop, his tools came by boat and Ben Barlow got him lodgings at the home of Cyril Simpson, a sawyer at Worksop's then premier sawmill Godley and Goulding. They supplied all the timber for the canal company's use.

Albert would bike home to West Stockwith once a fortnight to take his washing and see his family and friends and then bike back to Worksop late Sunday afternoon.

The main canal company workshop was at Top locks Thorpe Salvin with a blacksmiths shop, carpenter's house and workshop, a lime house, a derrick crane and a stone cutting bench.

After a couple of years Ben Barlow retired, his job being taken by Herbert Bagshaw, a carpenter from the Macclesfield canal. He was a very go ahead man and walked the canal once a week every week with the use of the railway. He told the gang that it would be the best canal in England.

They lifted the roofs of Worksop Yard stables and made a joiners shop and a blacksmiths shop. The derrick crane and stone masons saw bench were moved to Worksop and bays were built for sand and gravel. Mr Bagshaw was a great believer in concrete.

Albert had worked for the company for just over three years when new gates were needed for Misterton Bottom lock. They were always made in winter and fitted in summer; a good method. A stoppage notice was issued to all boatmen; stop planks put in place and old gates out.

Tommy Mountney stayed at the Packet Inn Misterton, Albert went to his parents home at West Stockwith and Mr Bagshaw and the Worksop men arrived by train for 07-00 parade. Albert was already on duty, but no Tommy. The landlord said his bed had not been slept in. They feared the worst. Tommy was always lighting his pipe and could have stumbled and fallen in; he liked a smoke before going to bed. The gang found his body in the sludge,

*West Stockwith Basin, the Tomlinson's Yard on the right*

Albert asked if his brother could have Tommy's job; he was a pattern maker working three days a week. He got permission to leave the site and call at Newell's to inform Harold of the offer. They worked together for thirty five years in spite of fall-outs!

They built steam dredger 'Joan', the work boat 'Norah' with full messing facilities, the ice boat and the pompeys. Harold was a skilled woodcarver and would always carve the date on the gate. I have never seen work as good anywhere.

Albert got married in the early 1940's to a West Stockwith girl, Elsie Flowers. He always said every time they planned to marry on a Bank holiday a stoppage cropped up. They were blessed with a daughter Dorothy in 1944. One of Albert's fireside stories was about the Rose Brothers of Gainsborough. They ran a barbers shop with four chairs. Their main business was early in the morning shaving men to go to work in the town. Their method was to lather the first man, then the second, then shave the first but only one brother worked. Customers complained for the delay on one side of the shop. They had a tobacco counter selling cigarettes by weight. The other brother was in a back room making a packing machine. The customers told the brothers to make up their minds what they wanted to do. They opted for the machine and became world famous for packaging.

In 1957 Albert and Harold built new low gates for West Stockwith by hand. This time the Horizontal Bandmill was operated by Edgar Clarke. All previous gates at West Stockwith were made and fitted by Claytons of Owston Ferry, a firm of millwrights. Albert retired from the cut in 1961 and I kept in touch with him till he passed on in his eighties.

# Blaggy

I was introduced to Cecil Blagg over a drink in the Peacock Inn in Netherton Road Worksop. It was known as the poachers' pub. The best way to describe Cecil was a rascal. He had a very poor education and was from the west end of Worksop, noted for its poachers. Starting on the boats in 1918 as a casual, his first trips were from Worksop to Shireoaks lime wharf loading lime with a shovel. An empty boat was too high to tip the wagons into. The lime was in small well burned rock. It did not blow about until it was cracked open.

Then a trip downgate to West Stockwith. Getting used to the job under sail to Torksey was very frightening for him. He had to operate the centre capstan on the forward deck, the boatman Jack Taylor of Retford steered the boat, operated the reefing line and shouted to Cecil to raise or lower the lee board on the after deck.

They stayed overnight at Torksey and delivered the following day to a Chemical works low side of Saxilby. They went to Lincoln for a back load but got nothing. They then had to take an empty boat back to West Stockwith where they were able to get a load of wheat.

The skipper told him, never take a sack of wheat for resale to poultry keepers. Take a bit from one or two bags. It will never be noticed. The same loader and unloader always kept a tally. One of the main fiddle places was Woodcock's bridge Retford. Cecil was a skilled poacher if he could not get a back load. He would visit Babworth and Osberton estates before selling the rabbits to a regular butcher in Retford. The skins were then brought to Worksop and sold to a dealer.

Cecil had a very bad speech impediment and a problem with his feet and always wore good quality shoes, Brogues, on his doctor's orders. His sister said to me if he was a bit strapped for cash she would help.

Sir John Robinson (Home brewery) owned the Worksop Manor estate. He was good to the poor and did not mind the west enders taking a few rabbits. Cecil had started lamping the game birds. The keeper told Sir John, who would not prosecute, instead telling the keeper to frighten him off. Cecil went lamping on the Welbeck Estate and got caught. He was sent to Lincoln prison for four months. He was a model prisoner saying he got three good meals a day and of course boneless meat; he thought he was in God's pocket. After three months the governor said he could be released but he protested saying he had another month to do. He got caught again on the Welbeck estate, the keeper again identifying him by the soles of his shoes but this time he got six months with no concessions.

Cecil picked up horse care when working with Pierce Hindley and when he was not boating or poaching he worked casually for Billy Moore, a well known horse dealer.

He always worked as mate until just before the last war when he became a skipper on Furley's boat 'Elsie'. His mate was a Worksop lad, Don Priestley. If Cecil got a back load to West Stockwith he got a lady to go with him so he did not need young Don. He shared this lady with another boatman.

When I got to know Cecil he was past his best and lived in lodgings with Graham Wallis, a gentleman who had lost his wife and was doing a good job bringing up his family. Cecil showed me how to set all the lines and sheets for sailing and splicing. He told me how to work out the length of the haulage line. Two boats together total 144 feet; take off the haulage head of 24 feet and this leaves 120 feet or 20 fathoms. Furley's issued 40 fathom lines to their boatmen on the Chesterfield canal. Men could buy one for a few drinks. Cecil, like one or two of the later boatmen rented his horse from Furley's.

Sadly Cecil passed away before he was seventy. He succumbed to gangrene. I always knew he was a rogue but he taught me a lot about life and I will always consider him a good friend.

# The Chambers Family

From time to time during my apprenticeship I helped the works painter Dennis Chambers, a member of the boating family; a family spread far and wide whose father had passed on. I did a job for his sister and she offered me his accordion and a tiller and haulage line. At the time I didn't need them.

I also met cousin James who had gone back to Hayton and, of course, uncle Jack who told the best yarns. Jack said in the earlier years they were a well off family with two and sometimes three boats but when he started it was a struggle for a back load; their main work at the time being coal and stone. He told me of a time in 1881 when his dad and three brothers Alf, James and Harry aged 18, 17 and 15 had taken a load of malting barley to Birketts at Tapton. They stayed overnight and the following day loaded coal at Norwood pit for a brickyard at Worksop.

They had a big pan of stew they called 'lobby' for obvious reasons, consisting of a poached rabbit, potatoes, carrots, and any root crop available. Breakfast was kettle broth or eggs boiled in the kettle. Some of the boatmen could afford frying steak.

As they came out of the Norwood tunnel a waiting boatman told them to clean up the horse saying; or I will tell your dad. After they had had their meal it was getting dusk so they fetched a tunnel flare and lathered the horse in paraffin. As it darkened they lit the flare and set the horse on fire. They pushed it into the cut and could not decide if it drowned or was burnt to death.

They had to bow yank the boat to Turnerwood and borrow a donkey to get back to Worksop. Jack never found out how they were punished.

In 1904 Harry Chambers moved from Hayton to Belk Lane lock Killamarsh with his family to be lock keeper. They were moved by the family boat. Harry's dad James kept the Norwood locks and there is a well known photo of him near a side pond using a drag.

In 1910 a boatman passing Jack's dad's cottage at Clarborough said to Jack's mum "if your Alf wants 'The Three Sisters' she's at Worksop Canal Company yard". Alf was working at Gainsborough Gas Works at the time but the following day he biked to Worksop to pick up the boat. Uncle James operated from the Shireoaks Colliery Company's wharf at Worksop with a 'gunnel' boat named 'Evelyn' and a Great Central boat. The family had the coal contract at the wharf for resale and also for the Bracebridge Sewage Works pumping station and several Trentside pumping stations.

When Jack and Dave started boating (Dave's real name was Alfred) Joe Beeston had the Company work (GCR) but had stopped trading at the outbreak of the 1914/18 war. His son Punch joined up, survived the war, married and settled in

*The Chambers family travelling empty at Manton Viaduct*

Dinnington.

Ben Barlow gave the Chambers brothers the Company work and when they eventually packed up Harry Clark got the work.

'The Three Sisters' was getting a bit tired in the head; it took a lot of thump so when they took a load of coal to East Butterwick pumping station and got the tide wrong they had to flood three fields to get from the pumping station arm back into the river.

When they got to Tomlinson's yard back at West Stockwith they asked William to splice on a new head. He declined saying they would be at the basin for six weeks and he could build a new boat in three weeks for £120. They declined his offer and came away

In 1906 William Tomlinson had to survey twelve boats for Furley's to purchase for their fleet. He received a small fee for each boat and, of course, some failed. The Chambers brothers didn't know that a boat belonging to 'Fat' Jack Hewitt was a failed one and 'Fat' Jack was working for Furley's. He readily agreed to sell the boat and the Chamber's brothers got a ringer 'Coronation' built in 1901. The name was changed to 'Ida' after Dave's youngest daughter.

When in use the oakum would work loose; if they had asked William he would have wanted a small fee to survey it again. They asked Pierce Hindley who told them she was built with green timber and chewed her oakum. They would drive oakum back on a regular basis.

Three Sisters was sold to Charlie Smith of Clayworth a No 1 who renamed

17

*Unusually this boat at Lady's Bridge Wiseton has a lady steerer*

her 'Valour'. When he finished carrying in the late 1920's he came to Worksop bringing his family, sold his boat to Harry Clark and started a timber yard. It is believed 'Valour' finished up on the Basingstoke canal

Jack said as a lad he had one trip up the 'Cross Cut' for road stone from Lady Lee quarry near Worksop. When they had Company work they had to provide horses for the 'Ice boat'. They hired Drug horses from Godley and Goulding. The usual turn out all in single file was five Drug horses hung in line from the boat with the two boat horses leading. He said Drug horses were better shod, in a condition of good health and corn fed with harness well looked after. Farm horses fed on corn and chop were poorly shod with harnesses fastened up with binder twine.

Jack said, on the 'cut' he was always happy in the early morning and loved the dawn chorus. When they took coal to the Trent pumping stations and stayed the night at Stockwith basin they could listen to the 'Stockwith nightingale' when he had had a couple of pints of beer. Billy Elliott, the Furley wharfinger with a back deformity had the most amazing singing voice. Next day he would spend time swearing at everybody.

As the pumps went over to oil engines on the Trent the Worksop Sewage Works pump became electric. This left just stocking their coal wharf and the Company work. Dave lost his wife about this time leaving one or two young children so he stopped boating and became the carter for Shirley Aldred the charcoal producer.

Jack went to Steetley quarry and retired from Worksop Corporation. 'Ida' was left at the coal wharf and was the last survivor of the canal fleet, being broken up in 1976. There was always a rumour that Len Clark and a lady lived on her for a while.

*Gainsbrough Regatta and Boatmans Games c1913*
*Four narrowboats are visible*

# John Macfarland

My geat uncle Fred was born near the canal dock in Retford. The yard and dry dock was operated by James Crossland who repaired boats, but he said he never saw a new boat being built there. They also kept a supply of household coal there for sale.

He talked of a family called the Caudwells keeping boats at Retford but I have never found anything out about them. Noel Caudwell, a mason from Retford, and later British Waterways Section foreman, said they were not relatives of his.

Fred told me a well known story that he learned at Grove Street Methodist Sunday school. It was the life of John Macfarland. He was born in Scotland in 1747 and worked as a cattle drover. He was a rough man, a bit clumsy, but a good fighter. He got a job with the navvy gangs digging the canal, mainly for the good money to be had.

When John Wesley came to preach in Retford John Macfarland fell under his spell. When some men booed and jeered John dropped one to the ground and the rest went quietly. Wesley told John, out of your wages, save a bit each week to buy a boat. To save his money he was to trust a non practising clergyman eg a headmaster. John said, not with a C of E parson, they give money to the devil.

When the 'cut' opened John had not got enough money saved so he had a partner on one early trip. They badly damaged a lock gate and were fined by the Company. You can well understand poorly trained men taking a sailing narrow boat on the river Trent. No wonder the local men called the crew 'cuckoo,' a local term for insanity. But John prospered and became a platform steward at Grove Street chapel. He married, had a hardware shop, two cottages and a wharf. Sadly, after his wife died, the business failed. People called him John Macfailing.

He refused the Rector of West Retford's offer of a place to live in Trinity hospital saying that he would rather sleep with the devil. He lived in the workhouse and barrowed coal from the basin to St. Swithins, but he never lost his faith and attended chapel until his death. A memorial to him is in the chapel.

# P Hindley and Son

One Saturday afternoon I went with my grandad to visit one of his gardening friends in Garden City (Kilton Road). As we approached the canal at Bracebridge a narrow boat was just clearing the bridge. The boat was well weathered with no paint or tar visible and also no name. It was loaded with coal and manned by two men wearing trilby hats. One was in front of the horse with a metal tool in his hand. The boat was under way and the man on board was coiling a rope round the chimney.

*A canal stoppage at Retford in the 1930's with what appears to be 'Ruth" on the right*

My granddad said it was Pierce Hindley and his son Joe. It meant nothing to me at the time but I was so pleased to see a boat. Years later, as my interest in the canal developed I would sit at the Peacock Inn and have a drink with Joe. He confirmed the boat sighting, saying the boat was' Ruth.'

She was the last narrow boat Furley's had built and was barrel bottomed with higher cabins, wider stem and stern posts and no halliard rollers. It was March 1949 and she was loaded with 16 tons of coal for Cockings brickyard at Walkeringham. The receipt was signed by Bill Woodhead.

Joe told me that when dad had his own boat she was 'Morning Star' and his granddad had Perseverance. She was all oak and a bit on the heavy side, built before Tomlinson's had the yard. Joe said his dad was very fiery and used some of the worst language on the cut. As a young man, fighting in the Marquis of Granby in Worksop, run by ex boatman Natty Beeston around 1900, Jack Taylor and Pierce were both fined half a crown.

Pierce was a well respected horse keeper; he knew all the ailments and cures. His last horse was a fine mare called Bella. When he worked 'Ruth' and Bella he would come from West Stockwith to Worksop in the day; this was confirmed by his last mate Stan Richardson.

Between the wars Pierce's wife Millicent was his mate. Unfortunately she slipped on the walk boards and fell into the hold. Breast cancer set in and she passed away. After Millicent's death, Pierce lost some interest in boating and for a time only went when he could get a back load. With the help of his two daughters Bertha and Fanny he set up a field gang. He would take the two girls out to the job in a float.

My sister in law joined the gang as war broke out. One morning as they waited to be picked up an army lorry drew up and a young man got out and asked "are you Mr Hindley's girls?" Bertha said "who's asking?" He said Mr Godfrey. Bertha protested but he showed her the paperwork and told them all; you are now working for Ministry of War and Agriculture at Gringley and Cornley Carrs. You will be picked up each day and brought back each evening. Still protesting they got into the lorry and served for four and a half years.

My sister in law learned to drive a Field Marshall tractor and a Caterpillar crawler tractor. Lily always said she had never heard of Gringley before. One of the girls, Rita Rose, married a tractor driver Harry Gagg and later kept the Crown (now the Waterfront) at West Stockwith. Harry also drove the mobile crane on the basin unloading keels loaded with paper pulp for Chesterfield.

Pierce returned to full time boating taking over 'Ruth'; Joe was taking coal to Littleborough pumping station on the river Trent working 'one hand all'. He was able to get a 'snig' (tow) both ways. They were both full time through the war and after but loads were having to be lightened to just 18 tons. Furley's put the men on daywork.

After the big freeze of 1947 Furley's men were told, when you return from Worksop put your boats on the offside puddle bank.

They bought two Leyland lorries; Big Bob Hewitt went on the Trent and later to Newell's. I once met him at Drakeholes. Joe went with his dad to Worksop on 'Ruth'. Pierce moored her in the Company yard saying she could stop there and Joe went to Manton pit.

After about 18 months Furley's sold 'Ruth' and contacted Mr Bagshaw who got word to Pierce to take a load of coal to Cockings at Walkeringham, along with Joe.

Without knowing it, on that Saturday in March 1949, I was seeing the last load of coal going 'downgate'.

# Cliftons

During my time on the cut I got one off jobs with British Waterways at fifty shillings a day. They had no boats and I picked up a bit of material carrying. Bill Ledger, the canal inspector, asked me to swap locks on Gringley lock house doors. I said yes but thought it strange that the Walker's had refused. I did not think that it was an eviction. Poor Ron Green had lost his mum and now his dad; he was a bit slow and did casual jobs on the Carr's. The bit of money his dad left him was spent on sweets and he did not pay the rent. He had all his belongings in two sack bags.

I swapped the locks and he told me he had only one relative who lived at Barton on Humber. He settled himself under the hedge and told me that if things got bad he could use a barn. After a fortnight my brother and I took a tarpaulin to put over the hedge but he was not there. A farm worker said he had passed away. Even today I still feel guilty for my part in the event that led to his death.

Years after I was working in the village, having my dinner on Top lock bridge and thinking of the past when a passing gentlemen spoke and conversation got round to the 'cut'. He told me that in between the wars he and his brother Charlie helped out on their dad's boat. He said his name was Clifton and his dad was George, who had sold his own boat to Furley's and now worked for them. He asked me to call at his home tomorrow and have my dinner there and learn some Clifton history.

The following day I called on James Clifton and he told me that he had traced his family back. Prior to the cut being built they were Trent rivermen. His great granddad bought a narrow boat and his son John and then George followed. At the time the Cliftons did regular trips to Spalding and crossed the Wash under sail and lee board, however they had to have a pilot.

It was coal to Spalding and a back load of potatoes for a wholesaler in Retford. George also kept the wharf and the Gate Inn at Clarborough run by his wife. One winter they were iced in at Spalding; the supplier would not split a clamp of potatoes due to frost.

Leaving his mate single on the boat George skated and walked home in three days; he skated to Bole marshes and then walked along the klondyke bends home. James never said how he got back to the boat.

George Clifton had a regular mate called 'Hooky' Billy who was born with just a stump for a hand. A few years before he worked for George Hewitt, the boat owned by John Hewitt who kept the Packet Inn at Misterton.

They were once caught out by a large Aegir when heavily laden with drainage tiles for East Butterwick on the early evening of the 2nd August 1882. George told 'Hooky' Billy to free a cross beam and tie himself to it which he did. The boat went under and 'Hooky' Billy saved himself. George, however, was washed up at West Butterwick, dead.

George Clifton had the tables of his pub bolted to the floor. It was very busy in the evenings and sometimes fighting broke out. Apart from being a boatys meeting place it was a very busy wharf. Around 1880 George got a job taking sand and gravel to Mount St Mary's school at Spinkhill for an extension. He took his boat to the 'warp lands' low side of West Stockwith where they could only load at low tide. It was all dig and pump. They had to repeat this operation two or three times to get a load.

They arrived at Spinkhill wharf where two carts and four horses plus carters were provided. It was a good pull up the hill and they had to hang three horses on a cart to carry 3 tons of sand and gravel. They would 'back take' the cart up while George was filling the empty one. The work in all took fourteen days and he earned 50 shillings, the most money he made from one job.

Eventually the family moved to Gringley where George bought a farmstead to store the boat gear, mast, sweeps, centre capstan and sail and became landlord of the White Hart.

Furley's needed 12 boats and he sold the boat thinking he could run the pub with his son, Charlie running the boat, but Charlie wanted a lorry and they bought one from the WD (War Department).

After WW1 he built a small fleet up in the 1930's and later, after WW2 he even got the job of moving oil from the oilfield around Beckingham to the oil terminal.

As soon as Charlie got his lorry George and his wife went back to boating. James, not showing much interest, and having a more secure job for his family.

When the Gringley bypass was built, before the last war, Holes brewery built the Cross Keys, a road house and George packed up boating to run the pub. Trade was dwindling and loads getting smaller.

James said his dad had a good business before the Great War even hiring a Great Central boat on occasions. He said everything was changing in the countryside as people bought cars, bus trips stopped and the Cross Keys closed. Charlie burned all the boat gear after the war.

# Mrs Foster

When I finished with the 'cut' I moved, with my wife, to Dinnington in South Yorkshire and she got a job as deputy warden on the bungalows. When I got home from work one day she asked me if I would go and put extra bolts on both doors for the old lady who lived next door, which I did. After about ten minutes the lady called me for a cup of tea and a slice of plum loaf. When I asked her; did she come from West Stockwith she asked; how did I know that. I said that everyone around West Stockwith did the same. She told me her maiden name was Hackett and they kept a shop in Misterton. She said a Hackett relative had a narrow boat on the cut. When he got married his father in law gave him a keel boat which he worked with his brother and a boy.

*Marion at Osberton Turnover bridge with brother Gerald steering and Jack Deane with the cap*

She told me a well known Trent story of two brothers and a boy who were taking Joinery timber from Hull to Lincoln by water. Water was low on the Fossdyke and they had to put half their load onto a lightening boat which cut their earnings after they had unloaded at Newsum's wharf. As they could not get a back load it meant a trip to Hull for nothing. They stopped for the night in Torksey and decided to go lamping in Knaith park just to make a few bob.

They got caught by the keeper, strong words led to blows and they beat the keeper to death. They took the body back to the boat and wrapped it in steering chains, which they would be using the following day. The boy was very upset so they invented a story and told the police when they reached Hull that they thought that they had caught a body in the chains.

The chains were pulled up but there was no body to be seen. The keeper was reported missing but his body was never found. The boy went out of his mind and finished up in an asylum, but the two brothers, when questioned covered for each other and got away with it.

The lady also told of a keel boat run by a husband, wife and son unloading in Stockwith basin. As the husband was coiling a steel hawser his wife stepped into the coil and it cut off her foot. She dropped to the deck without a murmur where she was given what first aid they could and taken to hospital, along with her husband, in the pony and trap used by the local doctor for his rounds. She still kept quiet, but that night in the John Copeland hospital in Gainsborough she screamed the place down.

She told me of the gas water boat, operated by Jim Pettinger, who took gas water from Worksop and Retford gas works to make ammonia and other chemicals at Morris's works on the Trent bank. When ICI was formed in 1928 Morris's closed with all the work going to Middlesborough.

One hundred and twenty families came to Dinnington to work in the newly opened gas works, including old boating families Elliots, Cliftons, Pettingers and Tom Kirkby who had been lock keeper at West Stockwith.

The lady said that when she was married at Misterton her husband Mr Foster, who came from the Isle of Axholme believed he was of Dutch descent and his name would have been Vorster.

# Herbert Cook

Herbert was born in Clarborough and upon leaving school went into farm service, becoming second man on a steam threshing outfit for Baines of Ranby. He married the daughter and ran a second threshing set for the family in summer. When work was slack he worked on the 'cut' with the 'thirteen week' summer gang, mowing, hedge and vegetation cutting. He told me he enjoyed the work. At the end of the war the threshing business packed up and, sadly, at the same time he lost his wife.

Herbert then took a job on the River Trent as relief lock keeper; he was given a full uniform (railway issue) and would have become a regular keeper; however a job came up on the Chesterfield canal for a lengthsman with a cottage thrown in at Bracebridge lock which he applied for and got. He had not been in the new job long when another vacancy, to drive a 10 RB dragline was advertised. No one wanted the job so Herbert took it and received full training. His mate and banksman was Ernest Wing. They were good friends as well as work mates and believed in the canal's future.

We once moved a greenhouse across Worksop for Ernest with a flat cart pulled by one of the boat horses. When I started to build boats I asked Herbert about renting a half acre of land which he had at the side of the lock house which he in turn rented from the Osberton estate. He asked me for 1oz of pipe tobacco once a fortnight to use it.

Herbert was by now in a relationship with a Mrs Catlin, a widowed lady. They married and went to live at the house in the Company yard and I took over renting the land from the Osberton estate at 50 shillings a year. It was called Crow Wood Gardens.

Herbert carried on with his dredging job but no matter how skilled he was with the machine the channel was moved over to the offside as it was on all the canals dredged by this method. A floating dredger was eventually brought in but it made no impact.

When the canal was 'made safe' in 1968, by lowering the weir crests, Herbert went wild and dredged the nine mile pond (Gringley to Whitsunday Pie) to the clay puddle. It has survived up to the present day without a breach and I would say that Herbert Cook was a real unsung hero of the old gang.

# Charlie and Freda Mitchell

Charlie was born on the canal side at Clayworth in cottages near the White Hart. His neighbours being the Ottley family and Charlie Smith, a No 1 boatman (he owned his own boat) who kept his boat nearby and whose family ran the White Hart pub. There was also a small blacksmiths shop

When the Smiths moved to Worksop and the Ottleys moved further up the village the cottages came up for demolition. Charlie had moved off into farming by this time. When we were boating Liza Ottley was looking after her unmarried brothers, both farm workers. We always passed the time of day with her and years afterwards when I was working in Clayworth I asked about her and was told she had passed on leaving her two brothers who could not boil water without burning it. A relative took them both back to Sheffield so that they could be looked after.

Charlie met and married Freda Wilkinson of farming stock from Langold and they settled in Bawtry and started a family. It was wartime but Charlie did not get called up due to the farm work. He liked a drink at that time and drove an Oliver 90 tractor, part of a lease lend. He had a very bad accident with the tractor while drunk and was banned from the road for life. After that he never drank alcohol but got a liking for fruit and nut chocolate.

When I got to know the family they were living at Forest lock house. Joe Wass had just retired to Harworth and prior to this Charlie and Freda were living in an old van behind the stables which was towed from Misterton by the British Waterways lorry. They were very easy to get on with and would give you their last penny. Freda did field work for Major Scott at Greenmile and always sorted her wages with the Major personally. She did weeding and striking and also worked on the static pea viner up at the farm.

*Charlie Mitchell fends 'Nelson' off the bank at Ranby 1963*

Freda liked a cigarette and when she was at home she carried a black cat on her shoulder wrapped around like a shawl. There was also a guarding goose called Lucy in attendance at all times. All the family did the large garden at the lock house and gave most of the vegetables away. When we were boating Freda would always make you a cup of tea with sterilized milk and some evenings we would spend a couple of hours with them playing Fan-Tan.

*Charlie Mitchell at Forest Lock House*

*Charlie Mitchell at work on the Babworth Culvert for the LNER, 1939*

Freda and Margaret, her daughter, would walk one and a half miles to Barnby Moor to catch a bus to Retford on Saturdays to go shopping and then walk the mile and a half back home with the bags of shopping. Charlie's main job was cutting the towing path from one end to the other, twice a year, with an Allen scythe. He was a good friend to the newly formed Retford and Worksop Boat Club. In those days British Waterways were sabotaging the 'cut' by dropping water levels and putting stop planks in at the head of Gringley, West Retford, Forest and Osberton locks to prevent passage by boats.

They had not, however, reckoned on the tenacity of those early boaters led by Bessie Bunker of the Inland Waterways Protection Society and Cliff Clark of the Retford and Worksop Boat Club and by organising regular club cruises the boaters were able to remove the stop planks, take the boats through, and replace the planks again with the minimum of effort.

Charlie would have insider knowledge of plans to turn off the water supply in advance of club cruises and this enabled him and one or two other members of staff who could see a future for the canal to ensure that the cruises took place as intended and the canal slowly returned to life, which of course did happen with the 1968 Transport Act in Parliament during Barbara Castle's reign.

Sadly Charlie and the Canal Foreman had an argument which resulted in his dismissal but the Boat Club supported Charlie and he was allowed to stay in the house. Not long afterwards poor Freda got cancer and died at the early age of 61 years. Charlie was never the same again, even when his daughter married and they came to live with him. At one time it was impossible to arrive at the house day or night without Charlie knowing you were on the way but now he often did not even come to the door.

When I next saw Margaret I was working with my brother on Hurst Road in Retford. She recognised me and showed me a photo of myself at the boatyard and told me that Charlie was living in a bungalow at Harworth and had permission from the Council to plough up the lawn with a Rotavator. I left the job soon after and never saw him again.

Both Charlie and Freda did their bit for the 'cut 'and I just hope that we will always have a Charlie's Lock in memory of them.

# Bill Ledger

Bill left the Priory school in Worksop to start work as an apprentice bricklayer with the well respected building firm of Tommy Houghton and Son. They could boast eight fine handcarts, kept well painted, with grey bodies, black wheels and all sign written. There were sunken boxes for sand and lime and at times lime mortar, ready mixed. The cement was classed as expensive and was always issued in treacle tins. The main jobs they did were repairing and replacing side boilers and converting middens to water closets for two foundries in Worksop; Hunter and Wardle on Tuesdays and Thursdays and Steel and Garland on Wednesdays and Fridays. Harry Watkinson was the bricklayer's instructor and the uncle of Reg Richardson who provided me with boat-horses.

My own father joined Bill as a first year apprentice as he became a second year apprentice but after two years left to play football for Grimsby Town. They were both called up for War Service. After the war Bill came on the 'cut' as a bricklayer and British Transport Waterways came into being. They provided a car for Mr Bagshaw, the Inspector, and Noel Caudwell was his driver while Bill took the job as Walking Foreman. On Mr Bagshaw's retirement Bill took over as Inspector. One

*Kilton Top Lock 1960. Herbert Cook (Left), Bill Ledger, Section Inspector (with dog), Bessie Bunker, IWPS (with Head Scarf)*

of his first jobs was to deal with a 'blow out' at the Willows culvert near to the nine arches (Manton Viaduct) which drained the 'pond' from Kilton Low lock to Batty's lock (Osberton). Bill always went to Said Mass at 06-30am and I used to make sure I was there then as there was always the chance of picking up a bit of Company work since Bill had got rid of the 'Norahboat' to the Argent brothers.

When Mrs Bunker and the Inland Waterways Protection Society came to the 'cut' Bill always turned out to help and was complimented on his gentlemanly ways and good manners. To me his only fault was trying to save and send canal monies back at the end of the financial year resulting in less being budgeted for the following year, something going back to his apprentice days.

When I needed the Blacksmith's shop which was in the canal yard at Worksop I put ten shillings behind the bar at the Canal Tavern. It bought eight pints of Tennants Rock bitter. However I did have to provide my own 'breeze' (small coal).

Sadly Bill took ill and died at the early age of sixty one.

*Lord and Lady Milton being loaded with warp at River Idle mouth*

# Herbert Bagshaw

I didn't really know Mr Bagshaw; when I came on the scene he had retired, but was still living in the canal yard waiting to move to Sheffield to be near his son who was a railway signaller. Herbert Cook was waiting to move into his house.

The Walker brothers spoke well of him. He had been a carpenter on the Macclesfield canal, coming over the Pennines in the early nineteen twenties to take over from Inspector Ben Barlow. Once a week every week he would walk the full length of the canal checking work done and work that needed doing using the local buses and trains. He repaired worn out edges of the towpath by shuttering and casting concrete copings using tons of cement.

He had his men build a new steam dredger 'Joan' and a work boat 'Norah' with messing facilities. Both were sixty two feet long. Inspector Bagshaw was a great believer in Blue bricks and several bridges were rebuilt with them.

He renewed every lock gate from Turnerwood to West Stockwith. Stockwith lockgates had always previously been made and fitted by contractor but now all the gates were hand made in Worksop yard.

Mr Bagshaw was contacted by Furleys to repair some of their boats after Tomlinson's ceased to trade after the Second World War and the work was carried out by the Walkers above Worksop lock and on timbers in the 'cut' bed under the Oaksprig Mill ( North Notts Farmers) where stop planks were fitted. As this process closed the canal it was only used for short duration repair work and emergency repairs. The Crosslands had a dry dock at Retford but this was thought to have been filled in in the 1920's.

He was a very strict Company man and carried out orders to the letter but sadly he could not keep traffic on the canal due to modern progress but I think he could be very proud of his achievements.

# Top Lock Folks

I used to get 'three day' contracts for British Waterways, either boat hire or boat operator. Cash in hand was £2-50 per day. If the job was done in two days the third day would be worked on Friday checking feeders, culverts and leks (leaks). My day started with a cycle ride up from Worksop, then from Cinder bridge to the Cascade clearing any rubbish from the by washes and weirs.

I met Fred Roberts, who had just retired from canal service, and he told me he had replaced Walter Guest who transferred from Moss lock upon demolition of the lock house. Moss lock was where most of the tools used by the summer gangs were kept as it was roughly half way between Chesterfield and West Stockwith.

The summer gang worked for thirteen weeks edging and mowing the banks. The local dialect corrupted the word 'most' to 'mostt' and then 'moss' and finally 'mossy' lock.

Mr Roberts showed me the bridge templates and frames used in the original construction work; the carpenter's house had gone however, and just one wall of the blacksmiths shop was still standing. He told me about the Alder trees that used to be cut daily by a Mr Wagstaffe to make Strawberry baskets.

Above the locks was the home of Derek Stiff and his family. He had two sons and made a living keeping and breeding pigs and also had an egg business. In the winter months we kept a boat horse at the Stiff's cottage, as work got sparse. We used to take feed up via Pudding Dyke bridge in Reg Richardson's Standard Atlas van, which was underpowered with the most awful gear change. One Boxing Day on leaving the bridge to go to the main road we got stuck on the hill due to a fine covering of snow. The only tool we had was a large screwdriver to prise soil from the side of the track to place under the wheels to get a grip. Graham Stiff, the youngest son still lives up at the cottage which has recently been badly damaged by a fire.

*Three of Furley's boats are ready to leave West Stockwith to travel up the Chesterfield Canal to Worksop c1925*

225.12.
Stockwith Bas

*Mossy Lock after conversion of tool shed into cottage*

One Friday afternoon I met an elderly lady, Mrs Blake, who lived in The Row and told me she remembered my family at Shireoaks. She was born at Top Locks and spent some years in America before returning to The Row. Her father, Thomas Hetherington, was lock keeper; Hetherington is still a well known local name. Mrs Blake told me there was regular boat traffic coming downgate loaded with lime. She recalled two of the boating families, the Beestons and the Chambers. Mr Chambers always boated with his wife and she and a friend were invited into the back cabin. She said the Chambers would never travel on Easter Monday.

Mrs Blake said a lightening boat was kept at Thorpe and one at Norwood and they were used to lighten the narrow boats when the summit pound was low in summer. Her dad used to walk over the tunnel and bring the Thorpe boat back through and she could recall him doing this numerous times.

When Mr and Mrs Roberts left the lock house and stables were pulled down.

*Mr Guest and family at Mossy Lock after the extension was added*

# Richard Furley and Co Ltd
## Hull and Gainsborough – Carriers by Water

Furley's started in 1770, doing coastal work as well as river work and had a dock and office in the London area. The craft were under sail; their keels on the Trent reaching the pinnacle of sailing for river craft equipped with Main sail, Top sail and Lee Boards, I believe of Dutch origin. They were late to motorise and ran a sailing barge, the Nar until 1949.

They owned twelve narrow boats on the Chesterfield canal to move the wheat from West Stockwith transfer basin to Retford and Worksop. They also owned Upper Trent keels that ran open-holded with canvas cloths when needed and also a fleet of Catches (Ketches). Their fleet was built at Thorne, West Stockwith, Gainsborough and Lincoln. At one time they had over 200 craft and when the Trent was improved by Frank Rayner, hired boats to the Trent Navigation Company and Fellows Morton and Clayton. The craft were built to different gauges to suit the dimensions of the various canals and rivers they operated on.

They took Canadian wheat to Bells Flour mill on the Grantham canal and imported Malting barley to Trentside maltings. The Malting barley for the Chesterfield canal was, however, mostly home grown. They also supplied Newsums with timber shipped from Hull to Gainsborough, Sheffield and Lincoln. Lincoln's Brayford was a busy place for Furleys. They took wheat to Dickinsons, Spillers, Hovis and Pollards and also Flax seed to BOCM where the boats had to go through the Glory Hole stern first to unload.

In the later years Furleys had problems getting back loads. I knew Charlie Espin and Dickie Addenhall, two of the Trent skippers who told me that everything was piecework.

George Thompson lived on Pillar House Lane, just round the corner from Furley's offices at Gainsborough. He was a horse dealer who attended every horse fair. In the later years Furleys bought horses from him and rented them to the Chesterfield boatmen. He also bought cattle and sheep and they always said he was the only man in Lincolnshire who lived off the end of the whip!

After the war things were not the same as lorries made an impact; the biggest problems for the boats being the need to hand ball the cargo and the lack of a return load. At the end of the grain traffic to Worksop in 1946 ten boats were in use carrying loads of 18 tons and with no back load Furleys could do more work with two Leyland lorries. They would tip at the Albion mills like a shuttle service and as the grain was loose in the keels they were suction loaded at Gainsborough. Floor malting was phased out in favour of drying out in rotary drums in factory units and all the waterside maltings closed.

As the fleet dwindled the skippers demanded a weekly wage. This was not forthcoming and they threatened to strike so Furleys sold the fleet. The wooden boats were scrapped and the steel ones went to Waddingtons at Swinton. They sold Ryton to Len Emmerson, a No 1 boatman on the Sheffield and South Yorkshire canal and when he retired a couple bought it to live on near Eastwood wharf.

Furley's bought Marshall's transport of Bawtry and all the lorries were put into Furley's house colours of yellow, black and grey. They did not have enough contracts and all the Canadian wheat finished on joining the EU. They finally sold out to Bradshaw of Sturton by Stow and that was the end of trading. I believe a sad end for a company of two hundred years transportation experience.

*David Bownes boatyard at Kilton Top Lock*

# The Manchester Sheffield and Lincolnshire Railway Company's Canals

## Instructions to Toll Clerks
## in relation to BYE TRADER'S TRAFFIC

The "Canal Tolls and Charges (Provisional) Order 1894 confirmed by the Canal Tolls and Charges (Provisional) Order Confirmation Act 1894,"contains the Classification of Merchandise Traffic and the schedule of Maximum Tolls and Charges and Provisions regulating the same applicable to the Manchester, Sheffield and Lincolnshire Railway Company's Canals.

1.  Fractions of a ton to be charged according to the number of quarters of a ton in that Fraction and Fraction of a quarter of a ton is to be charged for as a quarter of a ton

2.  Fractions of the first mile (that is when traffic does not travel more than a mile), are to be charged as for a mile and Fractions of a mile after the 1st mile are to be charged according to the number of quarters of a mile in the fraction, a Fraction of a quarter of a mile being charged as a quarter of a mile

3.  When the gross amount of a toll includes a fraction of a penny then that fraction is to be charged as a penny

4.  Timber is to be charged by measurement: 40 cubic feet of Oak, Mahogany, Teak, Beech, Greenheart, Ash, Hickory, Ironwood, Baywood or other heavy timber. 50 cubic feet of Poplar, Larch, Fir, Elm, Birch, Lancewood, Walnut or other light timber. 66 cubic feet of Deals, Battens and Boards as a ton (the latter being at the rate of two and a half tons per standard) and smaller quantities in like proportions

5.  Timber (except round timber) is to be measured by the mode of measurement in use for the time being. Round timber is to be measured by quarter girth and the division of 144 ( measurement being taken tapeover over the bark)

6.  A declaration as to the true description and dimension of timber conveyed and the cubic contents of the same is to be demanded by the Toll Clerk. In the event of doubt the invoice of the timber and a statutory declaration of the correctness thereof is to be demanded. Upon failure or refusal, after reasonable notice to furnish any of the aforesaid documents, the Company shall have the power to charge either the Consigner or Consignee or the Bye Trader according to the avoirdupois weight of the timber, to be ascertained in the same manner as the weight of other merchandise.

7.  Weight of other merchandise conveyed in a boat is to be determined according to imperial avoirdupois weight of 2240 lbs to a ton, and is to be ascertained

by the gauge of the boat. In case of dispute, actual weighing may be insisted on by the ByeTrader or the Canal Company, the cost of which, and of the necessary unloading and reloading, is to be paid for by the party in error, Toll Clerks are not to require actual weighing except in special cases and on instructions from the Principal Office

8.  NOTE where boats are gauged on the long weight of 2240 lbs to the ton, one fourteenth is to be added to the gauged weight to ascertain the avoirdupois weight of 2240 lbs

9.  The Toll Clerk must demand a declaration from the ByeTrader or other person, containing a true description of the cargo, and in case of mixed cargoes, a declaration of each description of traffic consigned in a boat, together with the respective weights of each class of traffic

10. Returned empties are to be charged in same class of the classification as comprises the merchandise which was carried in such empties when full

11. The wharfage charges set out in the Toll book are to be charged on all traffic using the Company's wharves

12. Charges are authorised under the Act for (A) collecting and delivering merchandise, (B) weighing merchandise, (C) the use and occupation of wharves for a longer period than necessary for loading or unloading, (D) loading and unloading, covering and uncovering merchandise,(E) the use of coal and other drops, (F) the use of cranes and power, or labour for working the same,(G) provision of towage for a ByeTrader,(H) use of canal berths, lay byes and basins belonging to the Company not alongside a private wharf by a boat beyond the period necessary for loading or unloading and (I) gauging and weighing boats. Application must be made to the Principal Office for the amount of the charges

13. Where merchandise is conveyed in a boat which passes through one or more locks on the Western canals or on the Chesterfield Canal of the Company, the Company may charge a minimum toll of three shillings, or where merchandise is conveyed in a boat which passes through the Summit pool at Norwood, on the Chesterfield Canal, the Company may charge a minimum toll of six shillings

14. Where merchandise is conveyed in a boat which passes through one or more locks on the Eastern Canals of the Company, the Company may charge a minimum of five shillings

15. For an empty boat which passes through one or more locks on the Chesterfield canal the Company may charge the sum of three shillings or for

an empty boat which passes through one or more locks through the Eastern Canals, the Company may charge the sum of five shillings or for an empty boat which passes through the summit pool at Norwood on the Chesterfield Canal the Company may charge the sum of six shillings, provided that such empty boat is not returning after delivering cargo in respect of which there has been paid to the Company a toll of not less than three shillings, five shillings or six shillings, as the case may be, or is not on its way to load cargo in respect of which a like toll will become payable to the Company

16. For an empty boat which passes through one or more locks on the Western Canals the Company may charge the sum of three shillings

17. If two narrow boats( whether carrying cargo or empty) capable of passing through a lock alongside one another pass through a lock at the same time they shall be reckoned for purposes of clauses fifteen and sixteen as one boat

18. No charge is to be demanded for loading or unloading over towpaths and canal banks( not forming the frontage of a wharf) provided no injury is done to the Company's property or obstruction caused to traffic

19. No charge is to be demanded for boats or barges tied up at night, or for a reasonable period when not at work if the traffic of the canal or of a terminal station or canal basin is not thereby impeded

20. Notice is to be given to the principal office of any boats which are not gauged and indexed, navigating the canal.

# The end and a new beginning

During the war time things changed, the pace of work speeded up and there seemed to be no relaxing with the war effort. Several old boatmen got jobs at Newell's, Rose's and Marshall's making gun turrets and machine guns for aircraft.

With timber on ration Billy Tomlinson did part time work at the boatyard and shifts at Newell's. Young mates from the boats became skippers and avoided War service. The boats got into a neglected state and were patched where they could be with chalico smeared on the defect and a tin lid nailed over it. Newsum's sawmill was only cutting timber for the War Department.

Bill Beighton and his brother in law Bill Major ran a boat. Bill Major put his name in the wet mortar at Kilton Low lock and it was there for donkey's years. A Mr Garside from the canal repair gang also took a Furley boat. The newcomers learnt by faults and mistakes as they went along plus a bit of help from the few remaining regulars.

Ben Ray came from the railway in the summer of 1943 to run the lock at West Stockwith. One summer's evening Joe Hindley showed him how he was the only canal workman who remained on traffic into the 1970's. Newsum's sawmill stopped work as the firm went over to mass joinery work for the big Council house projects: Billy's work was dwindling as wood was still rationed. Furley's asked Mr Bagshaw if he could order timber locally.

Three heavy timbers were dug into the canal bed under North Notts Farmers warehouse in Worksop. The 'pond' was lowered for the job as the coal trade now only amounted to three loads a week to Smith's mill. The Walker brothers renewed strokes to at least three narrow boats plus other major repairs.

The severe Winter of 1946/7 stopped the wheat trade; the ice boat pulled by seven horses, 2 boat horses and 5 farm horses broke through to Drakeholes tunnel where some boats and crews had taken shelter but the ice closed in behind them and it took three days to get back to Worksop

Furley's had put the crews on daywork; loads were now down to 18 tons. Don Priestly worked with Blaggy and they were tied up at Stockwith for three weeks waiting for wheat to come up river due to a strike at Hull. They had to 'strap' bread and milk from Redfern's shop in Chesterfield Terrace. Breakfast was kettle broth. Donny had to 'strap' the money for a stamp to write home for his dad to fetch him. Dad sent him a postal order to pay his debts off and he walked to Gainsborough and got a bus to Worksop and finished with the 'cut' There were plenty of hares, rabbits were scarce, but he really needed a lurcher and a good meal so Blaggy was beat.

Furley's got their two lorries running as boating finished. When Dickie Addenhall brought a keel load of wheat for Stockwith, Billy Tomlinson was tying up loose ends at the yard, ready to work on Furley's river boats, the same as 'Big Bob' Hewitt. Billy said "take it to Gainsborough, you will be given a pound for unloading it." When he arrived the manager said no so Dick told him what to do with his boat, picked up his kit and walked back to Stockwith. On the way he met a gang cutting and laying willow on the Trent bank; they offered him a job and he took it, later getting a job at Newell's and staying there until retirement.

'Big Bob' Hewitt also finished up at Newell's and got banned from every pub in the district. I liked the Addenhalls, Dickie told me that when he walked from Gainsborough he called on Billy to tell him what he thought of him and it nearly came to blows. I always got a slice of plum loaf when I visited him.

The last working boat belonged to Mr Travis, son in law of Mr Hill the brick maker. She was called Lord Milton and was operated by George Spencer with a hired horse. The boat was in a poor state of repair when she carried the last load of warp from Stockwith to Walkeringham in June 1955. Bill Woodhead signed the receipt for 20 tons. Bill left soon afterwards becoming a school caretaker. The boat, worn out, was scrapped.

*Reg Richardson with 'Dolly' at Bracebridge Lock, Worksop*

*'Lorna' horse drawn passing the White Hart at Clayworth*

I finished up building two boats for tripping, my brother Gerald went in with me and it was a successful venture. One was powered by an outboard motor and the other was horse drawn. We also got a bit of material carrying for British Waterways as they had neither lorry or boat.

Reg Richardson was an excellent horse man and always provided us with a good mare. We came through Greenmile lock (Forest Top) one summer evening onto Forest Top 'pond' and the blanket weed was so thick the horse could make no progress. Reg told me to take the mare, named Peggy, to Kennel Farm Barnby Moor which belonged to his uncle Ron, a butcher. He told me to be back on the job at 6am. I slept in the manger, Peggy had the loose box.

Next morning I got to the job as Reg rolled up with 'big' Jack Dean. We put Peggy in harness breasted up with Jack in a seal. The towpath was wide to the lock and together they pulled us through the weed.

British Waterways bought a 10RB dragline and Herbert Cooke was taught to drive it, along with his mate Ernest Wing. They lifted the Furley fleet from the puddle end (Weat Stockwith) one at a time where they slid down the bank and were set on fire.

The Walkers went to work at Cromwell lock on the Trent and fitted new top gates. Albert asked the man in charge Mr Jones, a carpenter/diver, if he could have the old gates to make a new top gate for Kilton Low lock as there was no allowance for new timber and the canal would have been in jeopardy. The gates were taken to Worksop to be stripped of all ironwork and nails. Godley and Goulding had ceased to trade and the timber was taken to Oates Ltd at Worksop for re-sawing on their Horizontal Bandmill operated by Bill Gilling. The sawmill manager was Cyril Stratton who used to run Newsum's mill and cut for Tomlinson's.

The Walkers, Bill and Cyril were all allotment holders and all old mates and the one hour job took four hours to complete. Albert retired a few weeks after and Harold finished the gate on his own and we took it down for fitting on the 12th August 1963.

Cliff Clarke started the Retford and Worksop Boat Club in 1962 with membership £1 and he fought like a tiger to keep the 'cut' open. They had already started to lower the weirs. A few of the work gang supported Cliff's efforts including Charlie Mitchell, Bill Ledger, Jeff Hawke and Herbert Cooke who could see a future for the canal.

I got on very well with Cliff; we rented 100 feet of wharf at Drakeholes. I'm sorry to say that we didn't fit in with some of the boat club members and one member was given 100 feet of the wharf in front of us and set up a rival trip boat operation. Then the boat club sent a letter saying that they would be putting up the rent.

By this time the canal was getting a little nearer to surviving closure and the local depot at Worksop acquired a 'Witham Flat' (a vessel about 30 feet long with a cabin, an area for loading materials and a small engine with the propeller offset to take advantage of the deeper water in the centre of the canal). I got three days material carrying (23.2. 65) and then did tripping with the horse and motor boat until late September. We then pulled the boats onto the bank and my wife set them on fire.

I thought I had done with the 'cut.' Furley's ceased trading in the early 1970's when the EU stopped the Canadian wheat trade and the boats went to Vic Waddington at Swinton. Ryton went to a No 1 (owner boatman) Len Emerson.

I never thought I would get involved with the Canal Trust volunteering but I have enjoyed every minute of it.

# Pounds and Turns

In the summer of 1964 I had planned out a half size Chesterfield boat. With the help of Albert Walker I got as far as pricing for timber with Oates Ltd. They said they would cut it and store it for me as my own place was becoming a bit vulnerable. Even then the iron futtocks second hand were too dear so they would have to be of wood. The following year things went wrong and I left the 'cut' and lost track of everything as people retired, moved on or passed on.

One Friday evening my brother and I had a swift half in the Clinton Arms at Retford, waiting for the fish and chip shop to open. As we left we were seen by Richard Allsopp and the following day he saw my brother who told him that we generally drank at the Market hotel, so a meeting was arranged. Richard came with Harry Richardson, mainly to see if it was possible to build a full size narrow boat and I said yes, so a meeting was arranged nearer home at the Lock Keeper PH. Richard told me he had measured 'Ida' and would contact people in the Canal Trust to see what could be done. In the meantime I wrote an article to the Trust on my boating times which seemed to trigger things off.

A group of interested people arranged a meeting at the Hewitt Arms in Shireoaks and I met John Lower, Christine Richardson and Geraint Coles for the first time. I told the meeting a boat was possible.

I had lost track of obtaining standing timber and home grown timber had many new regulations surrounding it plus all the local sawmills had gone out of business. Undaunted the meetings continued to take place on a monthly basis.

A trip was made to Ellesmere Port to look at Ike Argent's 'Dawn' supposed to be 'Ruth' but in fact turned out to be 'Norahboat' in a worse state than China. We could have used the ironwork when the boat was broken up but all was scrapped.

*'Norahboat' at Worksop in 1956*

I was asked to get timber prices and on 25th February 2005 I rang Stuart Summerscale at Keelby. I knew him from apprentice days, and he quoted £14 per cube for larch and £15 per cube for oak. He also had a Vertical Bandmill that could cut a log 60 feet long. For the timber required his price was 5,893.80. The money was raised by public subscription and the timber ordered at 16-40 on 13th November 2006 with a delivery of 3-4 weeks.

I worked at Manson's sawmill part time and I was given Polish White Pine dennages 8 inches wide because the fork lift driver said they were too wide. They preferred 3 inches wide. I split these wide timbers down and made 500 sheerings and 300 shutts. I was given utile offcuts and made 250 1 inch diameter dowels to pin the bottoms.

We now needed a site to build the boat and a place to store and air dry the timber. The foreman at Manson's gave me enough second hand timber to make the whooding stocks and some reclaimed hardwood for me to make three caulking mallets and a heel tree.

My good friend of 30 years Andrew Oliver provided a great amount of packing case timber for free from which I was able to make all the stocks to build the boat on; twenty saw stools, a steam box and trestles. Andrew was also able to get me an air tank off a lorry to make the boiler, a borrowed steam roller water gauge and

*Building the Dawn Rose at Shireoaks Basin 2011*

a gas ring was obtained and a plumber gave me a second hand header tank.

Richard was able to secure a site for the boat to be built at Shireoaks basin with permission from the Canal and River Trust in September 2010. The Trust arranged to collect some surplus Heras fencing from West Stockwith using their maintenance boat 'Python' to form the secure compound. John and Barbara Lower assisted the crew with loading and unloading. The Trust's work party assisted in erecting the fencing which included a guest appearance by Terry Berridge. The Trust also hired a metal container in October 2010 for the duration of the project for storage and also to provide the only means of shelter for the boat builders.

All the main timber for the build had been stored at John Lower's house for 4 years and Barbara lost 30 feet by 10 feet of her garden. All the shuts and shearings were also stored there.

John was able to get 26 iron futtocks from John Bayliss, an IWA veteran who has supported the Chesterfield canal restoration in many ways over the past 50 years. They were in a rough old state having been use as boat ballast, but for free and I was able to tidy them up in the forge.

I found a firm to supply 90 gallons of 588 Pine tar and Boiled linseed oil: J. Allcock of Gorton. Their sales lady Sally Shufflebottom was very helpful to us and John Lower collected everything in three trips.The turpentine was bought from Rustins. Mal and Christine Richardson bought the bolts for the main hull and an appeal was launched for flannelette sheets which was well supported by Trust members.

I collected scrap to make iron fittings for the boat and the 720  8 inch nails. It's a good job I kept the forge as I was going to dismantle it. A Trust member donated a stove for the back cabin.

Late November 2010 we had a heavy snowfall and the site closed down until January 2011. My son Paul gave me a hand to set up the whooding stocks and John Lower delivered 90 7 feet x 3 inches x 10 inches bottoms. They had to be trued up, 4 inch dowel holes drilled by hand and a caulking arris formed. When two edges were together they formed up a lead for oakum.

The first day six members turned up to work; we mainly used my tools but we needed more and an appeal for old hand tools was launched. This was successful and we got tip top tackle. Edward Travis and Mr Worthy donated two good kits. Paul and I were kept busy sharpening plane irons.

The bottoms were dowelled together seven at a time and the inside face trued up. Paul coated them with a mixture of tar, linseed oil and turpentine, known as boat 'soup.'

Andy Jessop and Roger Newton joined us; the shape of the boat was marked out and cut with a handsaw. With the bottom finished Michael Edwards joined us and the next job was to drill two holes at each end of the bottoms and shape and fit the stem and stern posts. They were both dressed with the adze and the whooding cut into them to receive the ends of the strokes.

The next job was to fit the keelson in four sections half lap jointed and bedded on four thicknesses of tarred flannelette. I crawled underneath to push the bolts through. (On the Chesterfield boats the keel went in last; gaps were left in it so that bilge water could be run through for pumping).

Boiling pitch was poured round every nut, dowel holes were drilled in the keelson ends and the stem and stern posts and as they were dowelled together and plumbed a silver sixpence was placed in one dowel of the stem post for good luck and a twenty pence coin placed in the other so the boat would always have docking money.

The next job was making and fitting of the two bulkheads, the frames fitting in place and then three thicknesses of boards as you need strength on the shoulders. Iron futtocks were then bolted to the stem and stern posts and twenty six iron futtocks bolted in the hold and twelve wooden futtocks bolted in the cabins, six of which formed timberhead futtocks.

*Dowelling the bottoms together*

*Fitting a steamed stroke*

The first stroke, known as the futting or bottom stroke, was then prepared; edges straightened, a caulking arris put on both edges and a scarf joint cut on one end of each, A member of the team came at 7am to light the boiler and raise steam and two strokes were placed in the steam box together. As they had been drying for four years they were only left in the steam box for three hours.

Each stroke was taken from the steam box and fed into the whooding stocks and as the stroke was pushed towards the futtocks it was, 'g' cramped into position. The timbers bent very easily; the strokes being fitted in pairs working from each end and then filling up the middle. After 24 hours they were bolted to the futtocks and the cramps removed.

The next job was to nail up through the bottoms 360 handmade nails 8 inches long. This was a hard, long and drawn out job and it took over a fortnight to complete.

Now it was time for the first stroke to be fitted; this time with 21 feet long x 2 inch timbers. They could cross the joints of the futting stroke which were 7 feet long. The same method of steaming as before was used and scarf joints matched to the centre stroke but when bolting up we used middlings; 18 inch nails knocked through the two strokes. I made them out of old road spikes.

The second stroke used 27 feet x 2 inch timbers bolted to and middlings driven into the first stroke.

Lastly, the top stroke used 21 feet timbers again. The last steaming operation was to bend and fit the gorings; the timbers that give the 'lift' from the

*Philip Whiffin testing his patent tilting cam system*

headledges to the stem and stern posts, a sort of bulwark.

We used recovered timber from 'Python' to make all the deck carlings, the cross timbers below the deck timbers. We put a nice camber on the deck timbers and fitted them to the futtocks; then made and fitted the hatch carlings. The first layer of deck timbers were 1.25 inches x 6 inches Red Deal and before the top layer, which was of Ash, two layers of flannelette, the whole screwed together.

The next job was fitting the shearings; a mixture of horse dung, sawdust and tar were mixed together until the consistency of best butter was reached. This was applied hot on the inside of the hull followed by a sheet of flannelette and then the shearings, fitted vertically and nailed to the strokes.

Then the headledges were fitted over the bulkheads and the coamings around the hold, the timber being Siberian larch. These were joined and platted with metal strips; the gunwhales fixed into place, half lapped and nailed. The timber used was Keroin.

A timberhead was formed on the stem post and a metal collar fitted which I made at home, finally a pin was driven through the timber. The six timberheads (four at the bow and two at the stern) were shaped above deck level and pins driven through. Both stem and stern posts had collars which I made in the forge at home

Both decks were sealed with pitch and it was then time to fit the deck screens which were finished with an OG shape at the ends near to the headledges. The hole for the chimney was formed, smoothed and fitted with a hand cut tin collar.

The timber for the winches was second hand from Manson's and one of the team shaped the three winch rollers and fitted the spindles and collars to the roller ends. Also the home made toothed gearing I made in the fire, together with their two matching handles to turn the rollers.

The boat is equipped with four wooden fenders at the fore end and two at the stern. A pocket is chased out of the hull and the fenders bedded in on tarred flannelette and bolted through. We then bent D irons round the fenders using an old floor board cramp.

George Findley gave us a load of offcut rope which was unpicked and each strand pulled through pine tar before being driven into the seams with a caulking mallet and caulking tools.

Timber offcuts from the strokes were cut to form five cross beams the widest being the luchet beam. All the ends were dovetailed to fit wooden patrusses bolted through the sides.

With the seams caulked we sealed them with pitch and then gave the hull several coats of 'boat soup.' To caulk the bottom Philip Whiffin designed a fantastic cam system to safely turn the boat to an angle of 30 degrees using recovered timber to make the cams and borrowing a number of jacks, from Taskers of Sheffield arranged by Sarah Stephens, to simultaneously raise and lower the boat. Timber props were inserted to enable work to be carried out underneath the boat. The bottom was tarred and caulked and the joints pitched and the boat lowered before the entire bottom inside was covered with boiling pitch.

*Michael Edwards using Billy Tomlinson's original caulking mallet*

The name holes were cut out and Richard and Harry started the painting. The team made the two pump cases and the pump siphons and cut and fitted all the scantlings and shuts in the hold. I put the cabin floors down and fitted the back cabin out with bed board, cupboard, shelves, seat and finally the stove.

The back cabin was then carefully grained by Sid White and all the lettering was by Nick Summerbell.

Andy Jessop made two beautiful tillers, hand carved from oak slabs. He also cut and shaped the sweeps out of 4 feet x 8 inch larch.

Finally (20th April 2015) the boat was jacked up onto James Hale's trailer as the cost of using cranes was prohibitive. I was not present, but the team all took part and on the following day 21st April 2015 the launch took place. Again I was not present, but the launch was successful and the name Dawn Rose was chosen to be unveiled at a later date by Sybil Fielding, Chair of Nottinghamshire County Council and a good supporter of the project.

The name Dawn Rose was chosen as respect for my late wife, Albert Walker and his grand daughter.

*Dawn Rose in sailing mode*

# Acknowledgments

I would particularly like to thank Richard Allsopp who advised, typed and proof read my manuscript and also provided many of the photographs.

Harry and Lucy Richardson for their help and advice in checking my work.

John Lower who provided photographs of Dawn Rose at various stages in her construction.

Last but not least for Alan James for the design and publication.

My grateful thanks also goes to the Chesterfield Canal Trust, without whose support it would not have been published.

Any profits from the sale of this book will go towards the maintenance of Dawn Rose. If you would like to join the small team who operate the boat, details can be found on the Chesterfield Canal Trust website or by filling in the form issued with this book.

# Friends of Dawn Rose

In the early 2000s, a small group of enthusiasts decided to build a Cuckoo boat. These boats are unique to the Chesterfield Canal. There was a big snag – no new Cuckoo had been built for 80 years!

The project was launched by an article in the Trust's magazine in Spring 2004. An appeal for money to buy the wood followed. This proved very successful, so the wood was bought and stored to season in a secret location for several years.

Serious work started in January of 2011. It was led by David Bownes, who worked on Cuckoo boats as a young man. He was one of the very few people alive with real working knowledge of their construction.

The task was enormous, not least because of the decision to use only tools that were available 80 years ago. 360 hand-made 9" nails had to be hammered upwards to secure the bottom beams. Planks 27 feet long and 2" thick had to be steamed and bent to shape. Vast quantities of pitch, oakum and linseed oil were needed for the caulking.

The boat was launched and named in 2015. Dawn Rose will be appearing at various locations along the canal in 2018, including horse drawn demonstrations; see our website for details.

# The Chesterfield Canal Trust
## *Joint us and help close the gap*

The Chesterfield Canal Trust is a charitable company run entirely by volunteers, incorporated in July 1997. It took over from the Chesterfield Canal Society which had been founded in 1976.

The aims of the Trust are to promote the full restoration and appropriate development of the Chesterfield Canal, and to campaign for the construction of the Rother Valley Link, a navigable waterway to join the Chesterfield Canal to the Sheffield and South Yorkshire Navigation.

Amongst other activities, we run four trip boats - Seth Ellis in Retford, Hugh Henshall in Worksop, Madeline at Hollingwood Hub and John Varley in Chesterfield. We also have an 89 year old ex-working boat called Python that attends waterways festivals and does canal clean-ups. Some volunteers have built Dawn Rose, the first new Cuckoo boat for 90 years, using traditional methods and hand tools.

Our promotional trailer, the James Brindley, travels far and wide informing people about the canal.

There are Volunteer Work Parties on the canal every weekend and often during the week. Our office is at Hollingwood Hub, which includes Katey's Coffee Shop.

We have well over 1,700 members, who receive copies of our award-winning magazine Cuckoo and regular E-Newsletters. In addition there are meetings, social events and lots of other volunteering opportunities. Membership is available via our website, which is a mine of information about the canal.

**Chesterfield Canal Trust Ltd**
Hollingwood Hub, 22 Works Road, Hollingwood, Chesterfield S43 2PF
email: publicity@chesterfield-canal-trust.org.uk  tel: 01246 477569

## www.chesterfield-canal-trust.org.uk